THE 2010 STAMP YEARBOOK

UNITED STATES POSTAL SERVICE

HarperCollins books may be purchased for educational, business,
or sales promotional use. For information please write: Special
Markets Department, HarperCollins Publishers, 10 East 53rd Street,
New York, NY 10022.

Designed by Journey Group, Inc.

ISBN 978-0-06-202433-6

10 11 12 13 14 ❖/WZ 10 9 8 7 6 5 4 3 2 1

Enhance your *2010 Stamp Yearbook* today by ordering the mail use
stamps featured in the second part of this book. For just $8.95,
you'll get 17 stamps and their corresponding mounts. To order
item #991004 while supplies last, call 1 800 STAMP-24.

Other books available from the United States Postal Service:
The 2009 Stamp Yearbook
The Postal Service Guide to U.S. Stamps — 37th Edition

THE 2010
STAMP YEARBOOK

COLLINS REFERENCE
An Imprint of HarperCollins Publishers
www.harpercollins.com

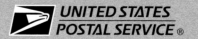

INTRODUCTION
Partnerships and Possibilities

ICONS  ARTISTS AND ENTERTAINERS

ABSTRACT EXPRESSIONISTS
PLACE AND DATE OF ISSUE Buffalo, NY, March 11, 2010
ART DIRECTOR AND DESIGNER Ethel Kessler

AMERICAN TREASURES: WINSLOW HOMER
PLACE AND DATE OF ISSUE Richmond, VA, August 12, 2010
ART DIRECTOR AND DESIGNER Derry Noyes

KATE SMITH
PLACE AND DATE OF ISSUE Washington, DC, May 27, 2010
ART DIRECTOR AND DESIGNER Ethel Kessler

COWBOYS OF THE SILVER SCREEN
PLACE AND DATE OF ISSUE Oklahoma City, OK, April 17, 2010
ART DIRECTOR Carl T. Herrman DESIGNER Robert Rodriguez

LEGENDS OF HOLLYWOOD: KATHARINE HEPBURN
PLACE AND DATE OF ISSUE Old Saybrook, CT, May 12, 2010
ART DIRECTOR Derry Noyes

CONTENTS

HERITAGE CULTURES, PASTIMES, AND LANDSCAPES

VISIONARIES LEADERS AND HEROES

DISTINGUISHED SAILORS
PLACE AND DATE OF ISSUE Washington, DC, February 4, 2010
ART DIRECTOR AND DESIGNER Phil Jordan

BLACK HERITAGE: OSCAR MICHEAUX
PLACE AND DATE OF ISSUE New York, NY, June 22, 2010
ART DIRECTOR AND DESIGNER Derry Noyes ARTIST Gary Kelley

MOTHER TERESA
PLACE AND DATE OF ISSUE Washington, DC, September 5, 2010
ART DIRECTOR AND DESIGNER Derry Noyes ARTIST Thomas Blackshear II

NEGRO LEAGUES BASEBALL
PLACE AND DATE OF ISSUE Kansas City, MO, July 15, 2010
ART DIRECTOR AND DESIGNER Derry Noyes

LITERARY ARTS: JULIA DE BURGOS
PLACE AND DATE OF ISSUE San Juan, PR, September 14, 2010
ART DIRECTOR AND DESIGNER Howard E. Paine ARTIST Jody Hewgill

BILL MAULDIN
PLACE AND DATE OF ISSUE Santa Fe, NM, March 31, 2010
ART DIRECTOR AND DESIGNER Terrence W. McCaffrey

PARTNERSHIPS AND
POSSIBILITIES

THIS YEAR, as the release of the Adopt a Shelter Pet stamps drew near, the U.S. Postal Service looked for new ways to reach the public—and found an enthusiastic advocate in comedienne Ellen DeGeneres.

"This is a subject that I am extremely passionate about," Ellen declared in March as she helped Postmaster General John E. Potter unveil the stamps on her daytime show. As a result, pet lovers and animal-welfare organizations mobilized; by early May, just days after these stamps were released, some post offices were already reporting that their supply had sold out. Although the success of Adopt a Shelter Pet highlights the continued relevance of stamps, it also suggests a less obvious but equally important lesson: the value of thoughtful partnerships.

Another colorful 2010 issuance was also born of collaboration. When the greeting-card industry found that customers were confused by the surcharge on large envelopes, they brought their concerns to the Postal Service; the result was a new first-class surcharge rate stamp featuring a monarch butterfly. As postal clerks begin to sell these stamps, greeting card companies will help make the public aware of them; customers will soon see the image of a butterfly on many large envelopes.

Thanks to an unprecedented partnership with the National Park Service, this year also saw the debut of *The Grandest Things: Our National Parks in Words, Images, and Stamps*. Illustrated with breathtaking images and historic stamps, this fascinating book showed that parks and stamps tell intertwined stories, with every page designed to draw new audiences into the beauty and variety of both.

The stamps in this book honor some of our greatest cultural icons, national accomplishments, and places of natural beauty, but they are not created and issued in isolation. Behind each stamp is a deeper story, one that involves collaborations between artists and designers, the passion of the public, and a partnership with you, the collector. As a result, the 2010 stamp program can properly be said to belong to everyone, from longtime enthusiasts to newcomers, including those who discover stamps through the satisfied purr of an adopted pet—or the sight of a simple butterfly.

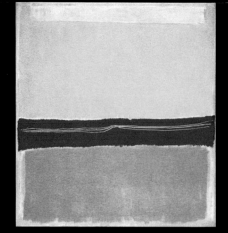

ARTISTS AND ENTERTAINERS

EACH YEAR, American stamps honor iconic individuals

whose perception and skill move us; in their work, we often

see ourselves anew. The word *icon* comes from a Greek

root suggesting resemblance or similarity. Just as medieval

painters strove to make their icons real, the work of modern

artists and actors reflects elusive truths about human nature

ICONS

ABSTRACT EXPRESSIONISTS

"The most interesting painting," Mark Rothko once said, "is one that expresses more of what one thinks than of what one sees."

During the 1940s and 1950s, abstract expressionists brought the United States to the forefront of the international art scene for the first time. Because their work comprised radically different styles—from still, luminescent fields of color to vigorous, almost violent, slashes of paint—these artists did not constitute a movement in the traditional sense, but they all sought to express complicated ideas and primitive emotions in simplified, abstract form. For them, art no longer depicted experience but became the experience itself. By emphasizing spontaneous free expression, they let personal intuition and the unconscious guide their choice of imagery—and forever revolutionized the world of art.

One of the most influential and charismatic art teachers of the 20th century, **Hans Hofmann (1880–1966)** pioneered a method of improvisational painting that linked the revolutionary work of the European modernists with the emerging American avant-garde. His use of color to create a sense of depth and movement helped shape the development of abstract art after World War II, as did his experimentation with different techniques and approaches. "If I ever find a style," he once said, "I'll stop painting."

Inspired by late medieval and early Italian Renaissance masters, the geometry of European cubism, and the expressive freedom of line in surrealism, **Adolph Gottlieb (1903–1974)** created a highly original, American blend of painting in New York in the early 1940s. His "pictographs," as he called these early works, aspired to a style of painting that could be understood by intuition, regardless of the viewer's cultural background.

Mark Rothko (1903–1970) created monumental paintings that probed the mystery of the human condition. His best-known works feature two or more color rectangles set within a field of color. Still and imposing, the shapes seem to float and draw viewers into a contemplative space that Rothko saw as transcending the mundane realities of daily life. Celebrated for his attention to color, Rothko used thin

In 1950, when the Metropolitan Museum of Art held a juried exposition to increase its collection of contemporary art, 28 artists wrote an open letter to protest the involvement of critics hostile to abstract expressionism. This Nina Leen photo of many of the protesters—among them de Kooning, Pollock, Gottlieb, Motherwell, Still, Newman, and Rothko—has come to be known as "The Irascibles."

ABSTRACT LIVES

IS HOFMANN (MARCH 21, 1880 – FEBRUARY 17, 1966)

ADOLPH GOTTLIEB (MARCH 14, 1903 – MARCH 4, 1974)

MARK ROTHKO (SEPTEMBER 25, 1903 – FEBRUARY 25, 1970)

ARSHILE GORKY (APRIL 15, 1904 – JULY 21, 1948)

WILLEM DE KOONING (APRIL 24, 1904 – MARCH 19, 1997)

CLYFFORD STILL (NOVEMBER 30, 1904 – JUNE 23, 1980)

BARNETT NEWMAN (JANUARY 29, 1905 – JULY 4, 1970)

JACKSON POLLOCK (JANUARY 28, 1912 – AUGUST 11, 1956)

ROBERT MOTHERWELL (JANUARY 24, 1915 – JULY 16, 1991)

JOAN MITCHELL (FEBRUARY 12, 1925 – OCTOBER 30, 1992)

80   1890   1900   1910   1920   1930   1940   1950   1960   1970   1980   1990

washes of paint, feathery brushstrokes, and radiant tones to infuse his paintings with luminosity.

Arshile Gorky (1904–1948) was a crucial link between Europe's modern masters and the emerging abstract artists of the United States. He taught himself by imitating great masters, then developed an original style that combined the lessons of cubism and surrealism with his own abstract approach and disguised imagery. "Art is a most personal, poetic vision or interpretation conditioned by environment," he believed. His daring late works—often shaped by the art and history of his childhood home—influenced much of the abstract art that followed.

Noted for abstract canvases of dense color and rich texture flowing in jagged abstract forms like geological formations, **Clyfford Still (1904–1980)** was one of the innovators of post-World War II painting in the United States. An influential teacher, Still worked with young artists at schools in Washington State, Virginia, and California and was a key presence in New York during the formation of the New York School.

Trained in the traditional techniques of European art,

Working frequently in collage, Robert Motherwell also experimented with a process called automatism, believing that an artist who allowed his hand to move freely across paper or canvas was able to plumb the subconscious and reveal the authentic self.

Willem de Kooning (1904–1997) transformed older traditions rather than abandon them. While much of his energetic and unconstrained work was entirely abstract, de Kooning's best-known paintings created a new visual vocabulary by blending abstraction and figural representation. As he once explained, "Ambiguity prevails in an art and in an age where nothing is certain but self-consciousness."

Barnett Newman (1905–1970) created deceptively simple works often characterized by large, even expanses of a single color punctuated by one or more vertical lines of other colors, which he called "zips." After coming up with the idea of the zip in 1948, he spent much of the rest of his career pursuing its possibilities. Unappreciated by art critics and the general public, Newman's austere canvases were a key influence on the color-field painters of the 1950s and 1960s.

Best known for his unconventional methods of dripping and pouring paint, **Jackson Pollock (1912–1956)** came to symbolize the bold new American painting of the post-World War II era. He aspired to make painting a direct extension of the mind and invented a style that allowed him to express himself in movement—like a dancer—and record his introspective train of thought as directly as possible. The immediacy and sense of freedom from tradition were new and distinctly American, and they helped place American painting at the forefront of world art for the first time in history.

Robert Motherwell (1915–1991) viewed literature and philosophy as integral components of his art and is generally regarded as the most articulate abstract expressionist. His works range from large-scale abstract paintings to light-hearted collages artfully constructed of labels, sheet music, and other ephemera. He is best known for the "Elegy to the Spanish Republic" series, an ambitious group of somber abstract paintings.

An inventive colorist with a style distinguished by large gestural strokes, bravura brushwork, and emotional intensity, **Joan Mitchell (1925–1992)** used complex memories of landscape to create and energize her expansive abstract paintings. Noted for many developments from the 1950s to the early 1990s, Mitchell's work is perhaps best remembered for its ability to communicate the visual sentiments of nature—or, in her own words, "to convey the feeling of the dying sunflower."

Before Barnett Newman experimented with broad expanses of paint, many of his best-known works included "zips," vertical stripes or lines that he believed represented a primal division similar to the biblical separation of darkness and light.

WINSLOW HOMER

Boys in a Pasture is one of around 400 works by Winslow Homer in the collection of the Museum of Fine Arts in Boston. In late 2008 and early 2009, the museum spotlighted several of his rarely seen magazine illustrations and etchings alongside well-known oil paintings and watercolors as part of the exhibition "Winslow Homer: American Scenes."

Winslow Homer paintings are beautiful contradictions. The figures Homer depicts are distinct individuals, and the world within each frame often feels as real as our own, yet each scene is infused with the sense of symbolism and universality an artist can convey only through a lifetime of travel and observation.

Born in Boston in 1836, Homer began his career in a lithography shop and later became a freelance illustrator. In 1859, he moved to New York City, where he studied at the National Academy of Design and worked as a freelance artist for *Harper's Weekly,* covering the Civil War as an artist-correspondent.

In 1866, Homer sailed for France, where two of his Civil War oil paintings won acclaim at the 1867 Universal Exposition in Paris. After returning to the United States, he devoted a decade to painting landscapes and country scenes, and his mastery of watercolor during the 1870s demonstrated the potential of the medium to a new generation of American artists.

Venturing to Cuba, Florida, and the Bahamas, Homer created oil paintings and watercolors of hunting and nature scenes, dramatic seascapes, and depictions of rural life. After spending most of 1881 and 1882 in England painting scenes of daily life in the seaside town of Cullercoats, he settled permanently in Prouts Neck, Maine, where he thrived on solitude and continued to paint until his death in 1910.

Boys in a Pasture, the 1874 masterpiece shown on this ninth American Treasures stamp, captures the depth, warmth, and contradictory spirit of Winslow Homer's finest works: an air of nostalgia that also hints at hope for the future.

A RICH DISPLAY

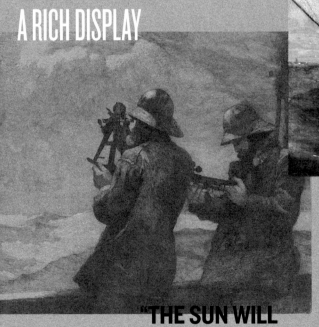

"THE SUN WILL NOT RISE OR SET WITHOUT MY NOTICE AND THANKS."

— Winslow Homer in a letter to his brother, 1895

Homer's 1877 watercolor *Blackboard* (below) highlights his interest in education, while the energetic oil painting *Breezing Up (A Fair Wind)*, shown to the left, has often been seen as representing American optimism.

WINSLOW HOMER ON STAMPS

Sharp-eyed collectors may have seen the work of Winslow Homer on previous U.S. stamps. In 1962, the U.S. Post Office Department issued a 4-cent stamp featuring *Breezing Up (A Fair Wind)*, a painting from the 1870s showing a man and three boys sailing. Homer's 1885 painting *The Fog Warning* was also honored on the popular Four Centuries of American Art stamp pane in 1998.

With the homespun simplicity that was her trademark, Kate Smith opened each episode of her radio show, which debuted in 1931, with "Hello, everybody," and always closed with "Thanks for list'nin' and goodbye, folks."

KATE SMITH

"GOD BLESS AMERICA"

In 1938, Kate Smith's manager asked composer Irving Berlin to write a patriotic song to mark the 20th anniversary of the end of World War I. Berlin reworked a piece he had written during World War I but never used, and Smith first sang the resulting song, "God Bless America," on *The Kate Smith Hour* on November 10, 1938, the eve of Armistice Day. "This is the greatest song Irving Berlin has ever composed," she declared. "It will never die—others will thrill to its beauty long after we are gone." During World War II, "God Bless America" drew standing ovations at Smith's live concerts, and today the song is often called America's unofficial national anthem.

For nearly five decades, the generosity and home-spun simplicity of singer and entertainer Kate Smith won the hearts of radio and television audiences. Known as "The Song Bird of the South," she recorded more than 600 songs, and her performance of "God Bless America" helped inspire the nation during difficult times.

Born in 1907 in Washington, DC, Kathryn Elizabeth Smith achieved early success in vaudeville and on Broadway, but her big break came in 1930 when her performance in a musical comedy led to the first of several popular radio programs. Throughout the 1930s and 1940s, she introduced her listeners to major new stars—including Abbott and Costello—while also becoming the country's most popular female singer. Her hits included "I Only Have Eyes for You," "The White Cliffs of Dover," and "Don't Fence Me In," but during World War II, "God Bless America" became her signature song. Through radio marathons, she sold some $600 million in war bonds—more than any other celebrity.

While continuing her work in radio, Smith made the transition to television. She started the first significant daytime television show in 1950 with *The Kate Smith Hour*, and she also hosted *The Kate Smith Evening Hour*, which aired in prime time in 1951 and 1952. She later appeared numerous times on *The Ed Sullivan Show* and was a regular guest on shows hosted by Andy Williams, Dean Martin, Jack Paar, and the Smothers Brothers.

Throughout her career, Smith was noted for her incredible generosity. She often visited the sick and injured, especially war veterans, and she donated her time to the American Red Cross. She frequently dedicated songs to orphans and shut-ins, and she responded to appeals for financial aid from her Depression-era radio audience. In 1982, four years before she died, Smith received the Medal of Freedom from President Ronald Reagan, who hailed her as "a magnificent, selfless talent" and "one of America's great singers of this or any other century."

COWBOYS OF THE SILVER SCREEN

LEFT: After making more than 300 movies, Tom Mix toured North America and Europe with his own Wild West show. RIGHT: Roy Rogers performs with the faithful Trigger in 1952. BELOW: Before becoming a screen star, William S. Hart toured European galleries and museums and performed Shakespeare in New York City.

WILLIAM S. HART
IN
"TUMBLEWEEDS"
story by HAL G. EVARTS, adapted for the screen by C. GARDNER SULLIVAN
DIRECTED BY
KING BAGGOT
A **WILLIAM S. HART** PRODUCTION
- a United Artists Picture -

For generations, the definitive heroes of the American cinema were cowboys. Brave, dashing, and fundamentally decent, they thrilled audiences with their adventures while serving as role models for young people. From the silent era through the singing era, the extraordinary performers who portrayed these cowboys were virtually synonymous with their on-screen personas; their larger-than-life talents helped make the movie Western an iconic form of American entertainment.

William S. Hart (1864–1946) brought a powerful presence and serious approach to early Westerns. Tall and trim, with acting skills honed by years of experience on the New York stage and in productions across the country, Hart became one of the most popular leading men of the silent film era.

Born in New York, Hart spent much of his youth in Illinois, Minnesota, and the Dakotas; in his 1929 autobiography, he described the joys and hardships of life on the frontier and remembered the Sioux Indians who taught him their language and customs. Later, Hart insisted that his films offer authentic depictions of the Old West and its people, from their clothes to their lifestyles and complex personalities. He went on to play the stalwart, tough-as-nails cowboy in more than 60 films.

Tom Mix (1880–1940) was one of the most celebrated Western film stars of the 1920s. He wowed movie crowds and live audiences alike with his daredevil riding, expert rope handling, unerring marksmanship, and rugged good looks. He also served as a role model for a generation of schoolchildren, maintaining a wholesome screen persona that involved "no cussin' and no drinkin'" by his characters.

Mix made his movie debut in 1909 and went on to star in more than 300 action-packed films, virtually all of them featuring him at his heroic best. In the 1922 movie *Sky High*, for example, he climbed the steep walls of the Grand Canyon, leaped deep chasms, dropped from a plane into the Colorado

In addition to being one of the most admired silver-screen cowboys, Gene Autry left behind a legacy that includes many hit records, a long-running radio show, and a successful television series.

River, lassoed villains, and rescued a damsel in distress. A legend in his own time, Mix wore oversize Stetsons, fancy suits, and handmade Texas boots with engraved silver spurs. He rode "Tony, the wonder horse," who also became an audience favorite.

For more than three decades, **Gene Autry (1907–1998)** entertained movie audiences and won the hearts of millions of fans with his distinctive singing style and easygoing personality. After beginning his career as "Oklahoma's Yodeling Cowboy" on a Tulsa radio station, his singing career took off in the 1930s, and he went on to record more than 600 songs.

In 1934, Autry appeared in his first Western film, *In Old Santa Fe*. Audiences were eager to see and hear more of him, and the following year he played the leading role in a 12-part serial, *The Phantom Empire*. He went on to star in more than 100 films, often playing a singing cowboy, and today he is the only person on the Hollywood Walk of Fame with all five stars—for radio, recording, motion pictures, television, and live theater.

Born Leonard Slye in Ohio and raised on a small farm, **Roy Rogers (1911–1998)** sang his way to stardom. With his warm smile, good character, and strong values, he always played the Western hero. Although Rogers found great success in show business, his modest roots kept him a down-to-earth country boy Americans couldn't help but admire.

In 1937, when Republic Pictures began looking for a singing cowboy, Rogers landed the leading role in *Under Western Stars,* a 1938 film that proved a hit with audiences and critics alike. In 1943, the studio began calling him "King of the Cowboys," a title that stuck for the rest of his life. During the 1950s *The Roy Rogers Show* was a television hit, as children across the country aspired to be like Roy Rogers and tried to live by his code of conduct, which stated that boys and girls should "be neat and clean" and "always obey their parents."

KATHARINE HEPBURN

As the daughter of a leader in the women's suffrage movement, Katharine Hepburn (1907–2003) learned early in life to take risks and challenge convention. Setting her sights on the stage while still at Bryn Mawr College, she headed for Broadway soon after graduation in 1928. Within just a few years, the role of a brash Amazon in the play *The Warrior's Husband* caught the attention of the public, earning Hepburn a film contract that propelled her to stardom.

With her freckles, red hair, preference for wearing trousers, and unique ability to draw attention to herself, Hepburn stood out in Hollywood. Sometimes she clicked with her audience—as in *Morning Glory*, for which she won her first Academy Award, and *Little Women*—but sometimes she flopped, too, as with the classic comedies *Sylvia Scarlett* (1935) and *Bringing Up Baby* (1938). Though widely admired today, the latter two films were a little too far ahead of their time.

After a string of commercial failures at the box office, Hepburn made one of Hollywood's most brilliant comebacks in 1940 with *The Philadelphia Story*, a romantic comedy in which she starred alongside Cary Grant and James Stewart. When the movie proved to be a hit with audiences and reviewers, it revived Hepburn's career, ensuring she would take her place among the greats of filmdom.

Bringing her resilient, independent persona to every role, Hepburn made more than 40 motion pictures, including *Woman of the Year* with Spencer Tracy and *The African Queen* with Humphrey Bogart. She received 12 Academy Award nominations, and her four wins are still an unbroken record for a performer. As one of America's most fascinating and enduring film stars, Hepburn was a role model for women who chose to live life on their own terms—and a true American original in her own right.

ACADEMY AWARDS

1934 Best Actress in a Leading Role *Morning Glory*

1968 Best Actress in a Leading Role *Guess Who's Coming to Dinner*

1969 Best Actress in a Leading Role *The Lion in Winter*

1981 Best Actress in a Leading Role *On Golden Pond*

"I WAS TAUGHT NOT TO BE
AFRAID OF ANYTHING."

Katharine Hepburn

USA
44

HERITA

CULTURES, PASTIMES, AND LANDSCAPES

STAMPS HELP US better appreciate the breadth of our heritage—from our ever-changing understanding of the natural world to the pursuit of perfection by our finest athletes. They help us re-imagine our own culture, in the words of poet Matthew Arnold, as "the pursuit of our total perfection by means of getting to know, on all the matters which most concern us, the best which has been thought and said in the world."

VANCOUVER 2010 OLYMPIC WINTER GAMES

In February, more than a million sports fans journeyed to the city of Vancouver, as well as to Cypress and Whistler Mountains nearby, to watch the world's greatest winter athletes make history. Surrounded by water on three sides and offering a gorgeous mountain view, Vancouver provided the backdrop for the unforgettable spectacle of the XXI Olympic Winter Games.

Vancouver was the second Canadian city to host the Olympic Winter Games—the first was Calgary in 1988—and the country's historic ties to the event run deep. During the 1920s, Canada was a proponent of including winter sports in the VIII Olympiad. The resulting Winter Sports Week, held in Chamonix, France, in early 1924, inspired nearly nine decades of incredible competition.

Many of the events at the Winter Olympic Games—figure skating, ice hockey, cross-country skiing, bobsled, Nordic combined, ski jumping, curling, and speed skating—date back to that first Winter Sports Week, but the athletes of 2010 also competed in Alpine skiing, biathlon, luge, and skeleton, as well as in the newer disciplines of snowboarding, freestyle skiing, and short track speed skating. After making their Olympic debut in Torino in 2006, both snowboard cross and team pursuit speed skating were again featured on the program, and the introduction of ski cross—a thrilling race down a technically challenging course resembling a motocross track—brought the total number of events to 86.

In keeping with the motto of the 2010 Olympic Games, athletes and fans alike returned home from Vancouver "With Glowing Hearts," awed by the spirit of athleticism and international unity of the Olympic Games.

THE STAMPS OF THE OLYMPIC GAMES

Featuring an illustration of an airborne snowboarder against a snowcapped mountain, this 2010 stamp continues a philatelic tradition begun in 1896. To help finance the first modern Olympiad, Greece issued 12 Olympic-themed commemoratives based on ancient art and architecture. Today, around 100 nations issue stamps to accompany the Games of the Olympiad and around 40 nations commemorate the Olympic Winter Games, creating beloved souvenirs to remember these memorable weeks of excitement and drama.

Whether enthralled by speed skating, figure skating, or ice hockey, millions of viewers worldwide looked to Vancouver as Olympic drama unfolded.

THE FOUR HOST FIRST NATIONS

Because the Vancouver 2010 Olympic Winter Games were held on the traditional and shared traditional territories of the Lil'wat, Musqueam, Squamish, and Tsleil-Waututh First Nations, the International Olympic Committee recognized them as official partners in 2006. From the earliest stages, local, provincial, and national aboriginal groups were involved in the planning of the Games, and the ceremonies and cultural programs reflected an appreciation for their contributions to Canadian life.

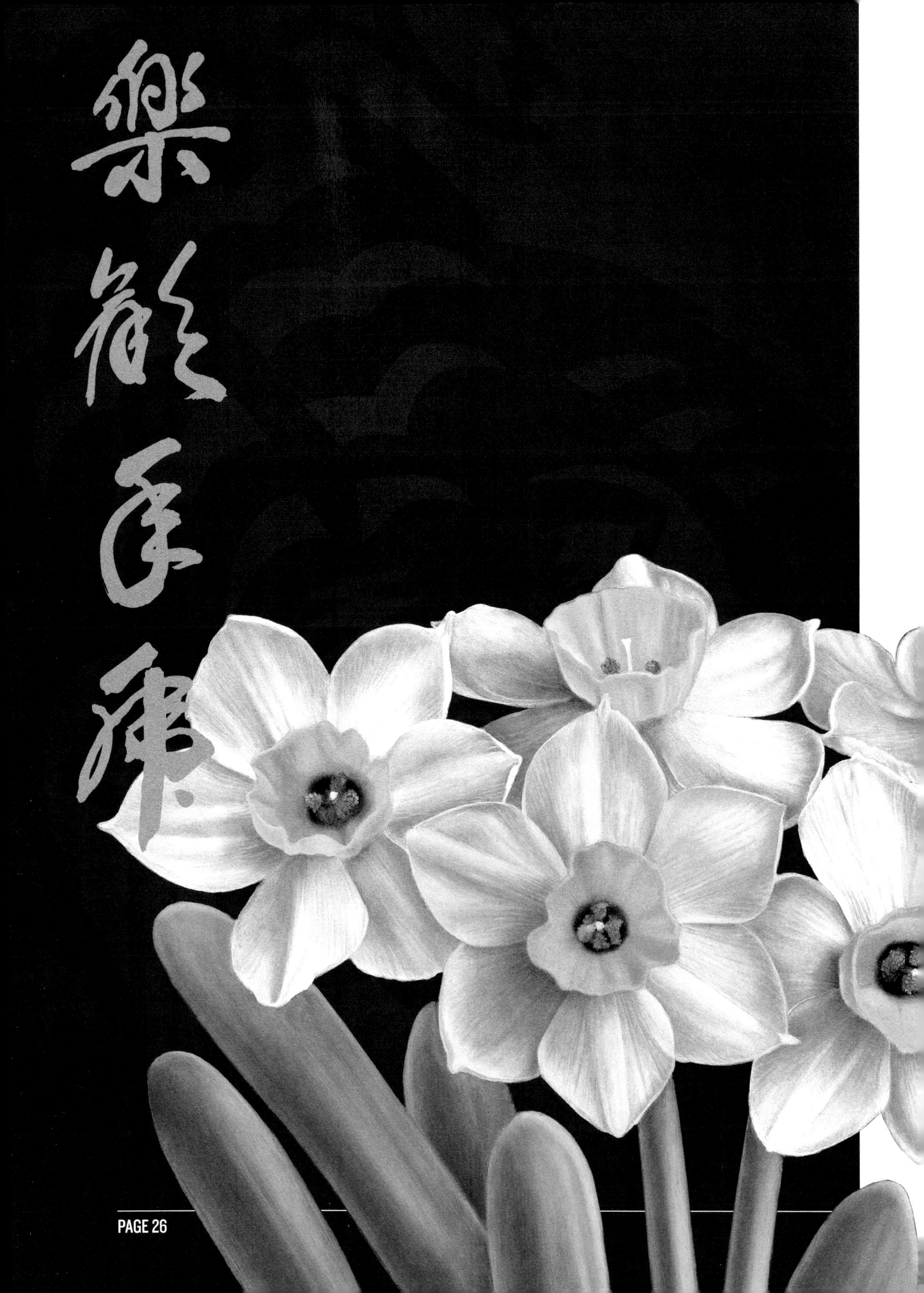

Considered auspicious all year long, the narcissus flowers shown on this stamp evoke the optimism surrounding centuries of Lunar New Year traditions—and the legends that nourish the symbols of the season.

One story, repeated by Europeans who visited China during the 19th century, tells of a father who bequeathed his property to his two sons, only to have the rapacious elder son claim everything but a single miserable acre covered with water and rocks.

Despondent, the younger son collapsed on the water's edge and lamented his fate. His cries drew the attention of a good fairy, who handed him three narcissus bulbs and told him to drop them in the water. Weeks later, when the flowers bloomed, villagers came from miles around to admire the fairy's gift. The young man whose future had nearly been stolen now grew rich from selling narcissus bulbs to one and all.

Hateful and ever jealous, the elder brother bought every narcissus bulb he could find, becoming so eager to monopolize the narcissus trade that he mortgaged his property to raise funds. He planted his bulbs across his vast acres of rich farmland and watched in amazement as all of them died— for narcissus bulbs do not long survive out of water.

Fortunately, the younger brother had purchased the mortgage on his father's former lands. In no time, he foreclosed on his brother and took control of the entire family estate. He then replanted some of the dying bulbs, just in time to see them thrive in the damp, rocky acre his foolish brother had dismissed as worthless.

Today, the narcissus is known to the Chinese as the "water fairy." Seen as auspicious at any time, its flower brings particular good luck when it blooms during the new year. Just as the younger son in the story was blessed with unexpected prosperity, all who celebrate the Lunar New Year can look to the narcissus with optimism and hope that a joyful future need not be the stuff of legend.

CELEBRATING LUNAR NEW YEAR:
YEAR OF THE TIGER

SUNDAY FUNNIES

Presenting an idealized portrait of adolescence, **Archie** focuses on a typical small-town teenager who is cheerful, polite, and well-meaning—despite his knack for goofing things up. Vying for Archie's affections are Veronica Lodge and Betty Cooper; meanwhile, eccentric pal Jughead Jones tries to avoid complicated relationships with girls, preferring to spend his time eating and sleeping. The whole gang attends Riverdale High, where their antics try the patience of teacher Ms. Grundy and principal Mr. Weatherbee.

Created by John Goldwater and visualized by Bob Montana, Archie and his friends debuted in the December 1941 issue of *Pep Comics* and first appeared in their own newspaper strip in 1946. A departure from the superheroes that gained popularity during the 1940s, they offered a reassuring view of the innocent foibles and mundane realities of teenage life.

A military strip with universal appeal, **Beetle Bailey** takes place at Camp Swampy, a fictional army base. Possibly the laziest man in the army, Private Bailey is expert at sleeping and avoiding work. While his chronic indolence antagonizes his sergeant, Beetle himself typically represents the common man trying to exist in the grasp of a system full of dense rules and regulations—and often comes out on top.

BEETLE BAILEY

Beetle Bailey debuted as a newspaper comic strip in September 1950. Cartoonist Mort Walker served four years as an Intelligence Officer with the U.S. Army during World War II, but he also derived his characters from real-life examples: Beetle was based on a high school buddy, while one of Walker's tough-as-nails sergeants inspired the character of Sarge.

Cartoonist Hank Ketcham was inspired by his own four-year-old son to create **Dennis the Menace,** which debuted in March 1951. A curious, mischievous boy, Dennis Mitchell tests the patience of his loving parents, ensuring that their lives are anything but dull, while also pestering George and Martha Wilson, the older couple next door. Competing for Dennis's attention are redheaded Margaret, who wants to make Dennis into a respectable little boy, and down-to-earth Gina, who accepts Dennis for who he is. Younger pal Joey follows Dennis's lead wherever he goes.

Initially a troublemaker, Dennis has mellowed over the years, and today his antics are more innocent than aggressive. Cell phones and computers have made their way into the comic, but little else has changed in this idyllic suburban world.

Garfield is an orange tabby cat who hates Mondays and loves lasagna and television. Lazy, fat, self-centered, and cynical, he makes no apologies, choosing to sleep all morning and eat all afternoon without guilt or shame. He lives with Jon Arbuckle, an awkward bachelor, and Odie, a carefree and energetic dog. Despite his sarcastic personality, Garfield does have a soft side, which he shows to no one but his huggable teddy bear, Pooky.

Jim Davis, Garfield's creator, initially wanted to focus the comic strip on Jon but soon realized that Garfield was the star. Although the perpetually cranky cat has slimmed down considerably and learned to walk on his hind legs, little about his personality has changed since he first appeared in newspapers in June 1978.

DO YOU KNOW
WHAT DAY
IT IS?

NOPE.
WHY?

OH, NO REASON. I WAS
JUST CURIOUS.

I SURE LIKE
SUMMER
VACATION.

WATTERSON

Featuring characters named after European philoso-
phers, **Calvin and Hobbes** explores the rich fantasy life of
a precocious six-year-old boy and his best friend, a tiger.
Lured into a trap with a tuna fish sandwich, Hobbes is real
only to Calvin; he is a stuffed toy to everyone else. Together
the inseparable friends take wagon rides through the woods,
ponder the mysteries of the world, and generally test the for-
titude of Calvin's parents, who never know where their son's
imagination will take him.

Calvin and Hobbes first appeared in print in November
1985 and soon became known for creator Bill Watterson's ex-
periments with creative layouts and fantastical—sometimes
distorted—drawing styles that stretched the limits of newspaper comics. The final strip appeared on December 31, 1995.

JAKE. After Jake, a Boston terrier, survived a harrowing journey from a puppy mill in Missouri to a pet store on the East Coast, his owners decided, belatedly, that caring for a dog was too much work. When he landed at the Animal Welfare Society in New Milford, Connecticut, a volunteer took one look at him—and it was love at first sight.

S helters take in several million dogs and cats each year; for lack of resources and space, half of these animals are euthanized. The issuance of these stamps highlights a more hopeful fact: The simple act of adoption could save many pets from this fate.

Unfortunately, many people wrongly assume that abandoned animals will have behavioral problems, when these cats and dogs are simply well-behaved victims of circumstance, such as an owner unprepared for the responsibility of caring for an animal or a family forced to give away their pet because of divorce, relocation, unemployment, or foreclosure. Animal lovers who want purebreds sometimes overlook the shelter option as well, not realizing that purebreds make up around 25 percent of the dogs in shelters; in fact, shelters house just about any kind of dog or cat a person might want.

Adopting a shelter pet is also economical. Adoption fees, which often pay for vaccinations and spaying or neutering, can run as low as $50 for a dog and less for a cat. Owners often find that shelter pets offer built-in convenience, too, as many dogs are already housebroken. Even so, ask the owners of adopted shelter pets what satisfies them the most, and they will invariably tell you that they love knowing they saved a life.

"Our local Animal Welfare Society now has a waiting list for pets to get in because the shelter is full," says Sally Andersen-Bruce of New Milford, Connecticut, who photographs shelter pets and documents their stories. Her photos appeared on the popular Neuter or Spay stamps issued in 2002, and she hopes that these new stamps will prompt more Americans to realize that adoption saves lives. "It's important to go to your local shelter or a breed rescue group to adopt your next pet," she insists. "You'll leave a vacant cage at the shelter—and help another unwanted pet."

FRANKIE. This distinctively marked cat and her two littermates were gravely ill when they were brought to a shelter for medical care. Frankie was adopted by the shelter manager—but was the only survivor from her litter.

ANIMAL RESCUE: ADOPT A SHELTER PET

PEACHES. After Peaches and her littermates surprised an elderly man by being born under his front porch, she found herself at the Animal Welfare Society in New Milford, Connecticut, where she and her siblings were spayed or neutered and given thorough medical care before being matched with responsible "parents."

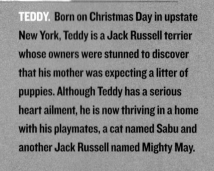

TEDDY. Born on Christmas Day in upstate New York, Teddy is a Jack Russell terrier whose owners were stunned to discover that his mother was expecting a litter of puppies. Although Teddy has a serious heart ailment, he is now thriving in a home with his playmates, a cat named Sabu and another Jack Russell named Mighty May.

BIANCA. Six years old when this photo was taken, Bianca was rescued after being hit by a car, only to be diagnosed with cancer; as a result, veterinarians had to remove one of her toes. Thanks to a program that allows senior citizens to adopt pets at no cost, she spent her final years in a loving, caring home.

TREVOR. A gregarious Labrador retriever, Trevor was abandoned with his littermates at a Georgia construction site when they were four weeks old. Two months later, after a stint in a foster home, he was discovered by a couple who had recently lost an older lab and were ready to open their hearts to a new companion. Trevor now swims daily in a Connecticut lake, and his owners' work-from-home schedule ensures that he gets the attention and training he needs.

A PHOTOGRAPHER AND HER DOG

Sally Andersen-Bruce doesn't just take pictures of shelter pets; she also adopts them. She tells the Postal Service that Brenna, her recently adopted nine-year-old Irish setter, has changed her life in amusing and unexpected ways: "The minute she lays eyes on me, she jumps up and runs over to me, while her entire body begins to wag back and forth, followed by a big puppy stretch as if to say, 'I'm glad you're home! I love you unconditionally! You are the most wonderful person in the world! What fun things have you planned for us today?' She puts the world back into perspective; I grab her leash, and we're off on a new adventure."

LUCAS. When this stray cat wandered, hungry and cold, from house to house, he ended up in exactly the right place: the backyard of a shelter volunteer. The Animal Welfare Society neutered him, made sure he was in tip-top shape, and helped him find a warm, well-stocked home.

Animal Rescue **Adopt a Shelter Pet**

BUDDY. This golden retriever was born with serious hip problems, which frightened his original owners into giving him away when he was eight months old. Adopted by an animal control officer, Buddy now enjoys regular exercise and spends his days snuggling with three other rescued pets and two very happy little girls.

WILLOW. The Animal Welfare Society found Willow one morning curled up in a cardboard box on their doorstep. The manager remembered talking to an animal-control officer who had recently expressed an interest in adopting a gray kitten, and Willow soon had a new home with three dogs and two cats—and a name that reflects her resemblance to a pussy willow.

"FOR THOSE WHO HAVE EYES TO SEE
AND EARS TO HEAR, THE FOREST IS AT ONCE A
LABORATORY, A CLUB, AND A TEMPLE."
—LORD ROBERT BADEN-POWELL (1857–1941)

Since the birth of the international youth scouting movement some 100 years ago, millions of children have learned to see nature anew while skillfully finding their way in the world. By discovering the leaders within themselves, often through adversity and adventure, scouts thrive on the lessons of nature, benefiting from what Lord Robert Baden-Powell, the Englishman credited with founding the scouting movement, called "a school of citizenship through woodcraft."

Historically, scouts learned to spot tracks and interpret their meaning; they also learned to read maps, navigate by the stars, and fend for themselves in the wild. A century later, scouts still learn these essential skills, but the movement has kept pace with a changing world. Coed scouting is now the norm in many countries, and scouting education has adapted to include advances in science and technology and new perspectives on environmental issues. Scouting has also expanded to include a wide range of hobbies and useful skills—from stamp collecting to financial literacy—but community involvement remains paramount. Scouts learn collaboratively, glean wisdom from adult mentors, and strive to become better citizens in the process.

From America to Zimbabwe, scouting organizations worldwide reflect their own national character, but their shared values are summed up in a letter that Baden-Powell left to be read by his scouts after he was gone. "Try and leave this world a little better than you found it," he wrote, "and when your turn comes to die, you can die happy in feeling that at any rate you have not wasted your time but have done your best."

SCOUTING

A DESIGNER'S VIEW

Created by illustrator Craig Frazier of Mill Valley, California, this stamp design evokes vistas that are as realistic as they are dramatic. "The small figure and landscape indicate very hard, directional light coming from low on the horizon—either early morning or late afternoon," Frazier explains. "The sky has that pale blue to indigo transition that happens only at those two times of day."

Although the large silhouette of a scout peering through binoculars catches the eye, a second scout perched atop a mountain draws the viewer inward—an effect that well suits the subject. Frazier says that he "wanted a level of discovery to be portrayed in the stamp itself."

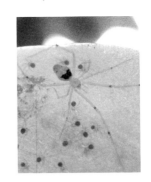

The tiny happyface spider may have evolved its curious markings to confuse potential predators.

NATURE OF AMERICA:
HAWAIIAN RAIN FOREST

The 'i'iwi, or scarlet Hawaiian honeycreeper, faces threats from non-native animals and plants.

THE NATURE OF AMERICA SERIES

SONORAN DESERT

PACIFIC COAST RAIN FOREST

GREAT PLAINS PRAIRIE

LONGLEAF PINE FOREST

1999

2000

2001

2002

This year, as the Nature of America series comes to a close after 12 issuances, this final stamp pane offers a glimpse of one of the world's most fascinating ecosystems—a place where most of the 20,000 native species are unlike anything else on the planet.

Because the Hawaiian Islands are more than 2,000 miles from any continental landmass, many unique species developed and thrived there. Six of the eight largest islands support rain forests, complex ecosystems characterized by abundant rainfall and high biodiversity. Like tropical rain forests on continents, the Hawaiian forests typically receive more than a hundred inches of rainfall a year and are home to many different species, although their densest concentrations of biodiversity are found in the understory, or forest floor, rather than in the canopy, or topmost level. Like their continental counterparts, Hawaiian rain forests are self-sustaining, with adequate nutrients recycled naturally among all of the plants, animals, and decaying organic matter.

The setting for this stamp pane is a rain forest on Hawai'i, the largest island, where the leaves and branches of mature *'ōhi'a lehua* trees dominate the forest canopy. Below, the lush understory is dense with ferns and saplings, as well as flowering trees and shrubs that add bright touches to countless shades of green. Colorful blossoms attract honeycreepers such as the scarlet *'i'iwi*, whose long, curved bill allows it to reach the nectar of tubular *hāhā* flowers. An *'amakihi* sips the nectar of red *'ōhi'a lehua* blossoms, while an *'ākepa* glides toward the same tree, where it will glean insects from leaf buds. A Hawaiian thrush known as the *'ōma'o* prefers fruits and berries.

ARCTIC TUNDRA

2003

PACIFIC CORAL REEF

2004

NORTHEAST DECIDUOUS FOREST

2005

SOUTHERN FLORIDA WETLAND

2006

Small insects and spiders are difficult to spot among the thick vegetation of an actual rain forest, but a few are visible near the bottom and center of this stamp pane. A Koele Mountain damselfly, for example, can be glimpsed clinging to a plant stem as a Kamehameha butterfly lays eggs on the leaves of a *māmaki,* its primary host plant. In its natural habitat, the cricket in the lower left would more likely be heard than seen, chirping and trilling from one of its many hiding places. Among the smallest creatures is the happyface spider, shown in extreme close-up at the lower right of the painting. Named for a pattern on its body, this spider is less than a quarter of an inch in size—not counting its legs.

Only one mammal—the ʻōpeʻapeʻa, or Hawaiian hoary bat—is native to the Hawaiian rain forests. Numerous wild pigs also roam the forests, but they descend from domesticated animals brought by settlers generations ago and are considered an invasive species. By digging up native plants, eating bird eggs, spreading diseases, and polluting water supplies, they threaten the rain forest community.

Hundreds of Hawaiian species have already become extinct, including half of the islands' original 140 bird species. Nevertheless, Hawaiʻi continues to be home to a remarkable collection of unique plants and animals, many of them still threatened or endangered. With the Nature of America series, the Postal Service has sought to highlight the hard work of conservationists while encouraging the public to appreciate the beauty of these special—and irreplaceable—places.

USA
44

2010

"JOHN ORCHESTRATES THE IMPOSSIBLE. THE ASTONISHING THING ABOUT JOHN'S WORK IS THAT NOT ONLY DOES THE ENTIRE PAINTING WORK AS A WIDE VIEW, BUT EACH AND EVERY STAMP IS A BEAUTY UNTO ITSELF."
— U.S. POSTAL SERVICE ART DIRECTOR ETHEL KESSLER

ALPINE TUNDRA

GREAT LAKES DUNES

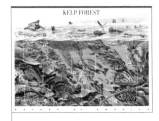

KELP FOREST

HAWAIIAN RAIN FOREST

2007

2008

2009

2010

VISIO

LEADERS AND HEROES

STAMP HONOREES amaze us with the scope and persistence of their vision. Uncommonly brave, they change the world not only through their own actions, but also by serving as examples who allow the generations who follow them to look at the world in entirely new ways.

NARIES

DISTINGUISHED SAILORS

RIGHT: An outspoken reformer and innovator, William S. Sims argued for better battleships and more accurate firepower at the turn of the 20th century.
BELOW: Arleigh A. Burke earned distinction first as one of the top destroyer squadron commanders of World War II and later when he helped modernize the Navy during the Cold War.

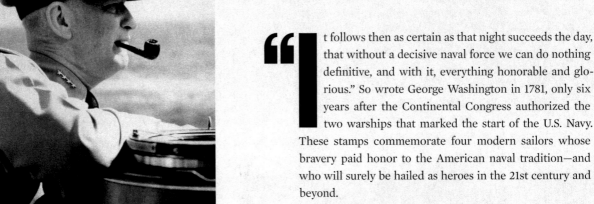

"It follows then as certain as that night succeeds the day, that without a decisive naval force we can do nothing definitive, and with it, everything honorable and glorious." So wrote George Washington in 1781, only six years after the Continental Congress authorized the two warships that marked the start of the U.S. Navy. These stamps commemorate four modern sailors whose bravery paid honor to the American naval tradition—and who will surely be hailed as heroes in the 21st century and beyond.

William S. Sims (1858–1936) helped shape the Navy into a modern fighting force. While serving as naval attaché to the U.S. embassy in France and the ministry in Russia during the late 19th century, Sims found European naval developments far more advanced than those in America. He

The first African-American hero of World War II, Doris Miller was awarded the Navy Cross in 1942 "for distinguished devotion to duty, extraordinary courage and disregard for his own personal safety during the attack on the Fleet in Pearl Harbor."

later implemented reforms, especially in the area of gunnery, while serving as inspector of target practice in the Bureau of Navigation and as Roosevelt's naval aide.

As commander of U.S. naval forces in European waters during World War I, Sims countered the German strategy of unrestricted U-boat warfare through various antisubmarine measures. His promotion and coordination of a convoy system dramatically reduced shipping losses and contributed profoundly to the Allied victory.

At the outset of World War II, **Arleigh A. Burke (1901–1996)** was an inspector at the Naval Gun Factory in Washington. His repeated requests for sea duty went unheeded until 1943, but after assuming command of Destroyer Squadron 23, "the Little Beavers," he quickly gained a reputation for brilliance and innovation.

In 1955, Burke was appointed Chief of Naval Operations by President Eisenhower. During an unprecedented three terms, he sped up the construction of nuclear-powered submarines and initiated the Polaris Ballistic Missile Pro-

gram. When he died, he was hailed as a "sailor's sailor" who defined what it meant to be a naval officer: "relentless in combat, resourceful in command, and revered by his crews."

After distinguishing himself in China during the Boxer Rebellion of 1900, **John McCloy (1876–1945)** won a second Medal of Honor in 1914 when American forces landed at Veracruz, Mexico. When McCloy directed fire at an enemy building, he drew retaliatory fire that allowed cruisers to locate and shell sniper positions and protect the men on shore. McCloy was shot in the thigh but remained at his post for 48 hours.

Described by one naval historian as "an almost legendary figure," McCloy later earned the Navy Cross as commander of a North Sea minesweeper after World War I. In 1942, long after his retirement, he was made a lieutenant commander by a special commendation from the Secretary of the Navy.

In 1939, **Doris Miller (1919–1943)** enlisted in the Navy as a mess attendant, the only job rating open to African Americans at the time. Two years later, when the Japanese attacked Pearl Harbor, he aided wounded or trapped shipmates on the *West Virginia* and helped carry the ship's captain to shelter. He then took over an unattended 50-caliber machine gun and targeted Japanese aircraft until ordered to abandon the bridge as fires raged out of control.

As a result of his bravery, Miller became the best-known enlisted sailor of World War II and the war's first African-American hero. He was later killed during the invasion of the Gilbert Islands, but not before playing a crucial role in the campaign for racial equality in the U.S. military.

OSCAR MICHEAUX

A mbitious, even visionary, Oscar Micheaux was a man ahead of his time. Born in 1884 to a farming family in southwestern Illinois, he went on to write, direct, produce, and distribute more than 40 movies during the first half of the 20th century, long before African-American filmmakers enjoyed industry support or widespread venues for their work.

Micheaux's films were often rooted in his own experiences. As a young man, he worked a variety of jobs, including a stint as a Pullman porter, before purchasing land in South Dakota and becoming a homesteader. In 1913, he turned his own experiences into his *The Conquest,* the first of several novels. As he traveled the country selling his books, Micheaux cultivated an entrepreneurial spirit that foreshadowed his career as a filmmaker.

In 1919, Micheaux earned rave reviews in the Chicago press after he wrote, directed, and produced a big-screen adaptation of his 1917 novel *The Homesteader,* which combined a love story, a Western, and a dramatic tale of African-American life. During the 1920s, he made more than 20 movies about such controversial subjects as mob violence, lynching, and racial identity. He also adapted novels, produced courtroom dramas, and dabbled in autobiography. Later, he became the only producer of silent movies for African Americans who made the transition to producing sound pictures.

Forgotten after his death in 1951, Micheaux was rediscovered in the late 1960s by South Dakota historians and again in the 1970s by film historians who were intrigued by early black cinema. In 1986, he was posthumously awarded a special Directors Guild of America award, and in 1995 the Producers Guild of America established the Oscar Micheaux Award to honor "an individual or individuals whose achievements in film and television have been accomplished despite difficult odds."

Micheaux himself would no doubt be pleased by recognition of his artistry and honored to represent early African-American cinema. As he explained in 1947, "We want to see our lives dramatized on the screen as we are living it, the same as other peoples, the world over."

Although his films often depicted characters who gambled, drank, took drugs, or used vulgar language, Micheaux made sure they also implicitly advocated the value of education and hard work.

MICHEAUX, UNCONQUERED

This 33rd stamp in the Black Heritage series features artwork by Gary Kelley based on one of the few surviving photographs of Micheaux: a portrait from his 1913 novel *The Conquest* showing a young, determined filmmaker eager to discuss and promote his portrayals of the African-American experience.

OSCAR MICHEAUX, HOMESTEADER

In 1911, after spending seven years as a farmer in South Dakota, Oscar Micheaux published an article in the *Chicago Defender* encouraging African Americans to go west and seek their fortunes on the frontier. Both haunted and fascinated by his South Dakota years, Micheaux vividly recreated his homesteading experiences in novels and films.

MOTHER TERESA

"IN ORDER TO
UNDERSTAND
AND HELP
THOSE WHO
HAVE NOTHING,
WE MUST LIVE
LIKE THEM."

Noted for her compassion toward the poor and suffering, Mother Teresa (1910–1997), a diminutive Roman Catholic nun and honorary U.S. citizen, served the sick and destitute of India and the world for nearly 50 years. Her humility and compassion, as well as her respect for the innate worth and dignity of humankind, inspired people of all ages and backgrounds to work on behalf of the world's poorest populations.

An ethnic Albanian, Mother Teresa was born Agnes Gonxha Bojaxhiu in Skopje in what is now the Republic of Macedonia. Drawn to the religious life as a young girl, she left her home at 18 to serve as a Roman Catholic missionary in India. Having adopted the name of Sister Mary Teresa, she arrived in India in 1929, and two years later she took temporary vows as a nun before transferring to a convent in Calcutta. She became known as Mother Teresa in 1937, when she took her final vows.

Following a divine inspiration and deeply moved by the poverty and suffering she saw in the streets of Calcutta, Mother Teresa left her teaching post at the convent in 1948 to devote herself completely to the city's indigent residents. Two years later, she founded her own congregation, the Missionaries of Charity. Centered in Calcutta, the Missionaries of Charity operated leprosy clinics, orphanages, nurseries, schools for impoverished children, and medical dispensaries for the sick and diseased. In 1959, she extended the work of the Missionaries of Charity beyond Calcutta, and in 1965 she established the first foundation outside India.

When Mother Teresa accepted the 1979 Nobel Peace Prize, she did so "in the name of the poor, the hungry, the sick and the lonely," and convinced the organizers to donate to the needy the money normally used to fund the awards banquet. Inspired by her example of selfless humanitarian care, today thousands of religious and lay people labor worldwide on behalf of the poor and the dying destitute.

Mother Teresa is shown here in 1974 cradling a child in a **Calcutta** orphanage.

ABOUT THE ARTIST

Known for his dramatic lighting and sensitivity to mood, Thomas Blackshear II has created artwork for 20 previous U.S. stamps as well as 28 portraits for *I Have a Dream*, the 1992 Black Heritage commemorative book. As a commercial artist, he has produced illustrations for posters, collectors' plates, magazines, greeting cards, calendars, books, and advertising. In recent years, he has also earned acclaim for his collectible figurines and inspirational prints.

For much of the 19th century, African Americans played baseball with and against whites, but by the 1890s most white team owners had informally agreed to bar black players. As a result, dozens of all-black squads formed across the country. In 1920, Andrew "Rube" Foster founded the first successful league of African-American teams, the National Negro League, which drew record crowds and profits in its first three years while encouraging economic development in African-American neighborhoods. Other leagues formed, and the first Negro League World Series took place in October 1924.

Despite the growing success, players in the Negro leagues found life difficult. Most teams engaged in barnstorming, the practice of playing local teams in one town after another, a financial necessity that led to rigorous, year-round schedules.

While on the road, athletes also encountered discrimination and racism in hotels and restaurants. Although they did not consider themselves activists, their persistence began to challenge prevailing racist attitudes and practices.

After ill health forced Rube Foster to retire in 1926, the National Negro League faltered, and the Great Depression forced many black teams to fold. By 1932, no major Negro baseball league operated in the U.S., but new owners emerged

Faced with exhausting, year-round schedules, teams in the Negro Leagues played nearly every day, sometimes two or three times per day, in all weather conditions.

THE MANY LEAGUES

to keep professional black baseball from disappearing entirely. By the late 1940s, the Negro leagues were an integral part of African-American life and had become one of the most successful black businesses in the country.

In 1947, at the peak of Negro leagues popularity, Jackie Robinson broke though the "color line" when he began to play for the Brooklyn Dodgers. More players from the Negro leagues were soon signed to white teams, and their loyal fans turned their attention to major league ball. The Negro leagues slowly dissolved, but today their legacy is undeniable. Drawing some of the most remarkable athletes ever to play baseball, they galvanized African-American communities, challenged prevailing racist notions of athletic superiority, and ultimately sparked the integration of American sports.

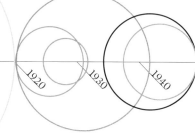

NEGRO LEAGUES BASEBALL

TOP: Josh Gibson slides into home at Comiskey Park during the 12th annual East-West All-Star Game on August 13, 1944. BACKGROUND: Rube Foster bats for the Leland Giants in Chicago in 1909.

THE FATHER OF NEGRO LEAGUES BASEBALL

Earning his nickname after defeating major-league pitcher George Edward "Rube" Waddell in 1902, pitcher Andrew "Rube" Foster (1879-1930) founded the Negro National League in 1920. He served as president of the league until 1926 and established its slogan, "We are the ship, all else the sea." Today he is remembered as the father of Negro leagues baseball, and in 1981 the National Baseball Hall of Fame recognized him as the leagues' "foremost manager and executive."

A revolutionary writer, thinker, and activist, Julia de Burgos (1914–1953) probed issues of love, feminism, and political and personal freedom in more than 200 poems. Her groundbreaking works speak powerfully to women, minorities, the poor, and the dispossessed, urging them to find their own true selves.

The eldest of 13 children, de Burgos was born in Carolina, Puerto Rico, and grew up along the Río Grande de Loíza. Despite her family's poverty, she graduated from the University of Puerto Rico in 1933 with a two-year teaching degree, later working at a series of teaching and journalism jobs while publishing poems in journals and newspapers. Her first collection, *Poemas exactos a mí misma (Exact Poems to Myself)*, included her most famous work, "Río Grande de Loíza," a love song to the river of her childhood.

In 1938, de Burgos published *Poema en veinte surcos (Poem in Twenty Furrows)*, a collection that confronted traditional images of women and addressed political themes, while the award-winning *Canción de la verdad sencilla (Song of the Simple Truth)*, published the following year, consisted primarily of love poetry. "[H]ay mil pájaros vivos en mi alma"—"[T]here are a thousand birds alive in my soul," she wrote in the lyrical, almost mystical "Noche de amor en tres cantos" ("Night of Love in Three Cantos").

In 1940, de Burgos left Puerto Rico for New York City and then moved to Cuba, where she stayed until 1942. Returning to New York City, she had trouble finding well-paid jobs in either journalism or teaching, possibly because of discrimination. The poems in her posthumously published *El mar y tú (The Sea and You)* poignantly document her loneliness and isolation. By highlighting the importance of community and solidarity for Puerto Ricans while also speaking to all immigrants, de Burgos fulfilled her calling as a poet, linking her own intimate emotions to broader questions of universal human experience.

LITERARY ARTS:
JULIA DE BURGOS

LEFT: De Burgos is shown here with Dr. Juan Isidro Jimenés Grullón, who called her "a poetic figure of great sensibility." **OPPOSITE PAGE:** In 1946, de Burgos received a literary award for her essay "Ser o no ser es la divisa" ("To Be or Not To Be Is the Motto").

"MY CHILDHOOD WAS ALL
A POEM IN THE RIVER, AND
A RIVER IN THE POEM OF MY
FIRST DREAMS."

MAULDIN AFTER THE WAR

After World War II, Mauldin temporarily retired from cartooning. He acted in two films, covered the Korean War for *Collier's*, and made an unsuccessful run for Congress. In 1958, he took a job as a cartoonist for the *St. Louis Post-Dispatch* and won his second Pulitzer Prize for a cartoon portraying Boris Pasternak, author of *Doctor Zhivago*, as a Soviet prisoner, saying: "I won the Nobel Prize for Literature. What was your crime?" In 1962, Mauldin joined the staff of the *Chicago Sun-Times* and was later sent to observe the war in Vietnam firsthand.

BILL MAULDIN 44
USA

Pencil ever at the ready, Mauldin sketches the likeness of Private Robert L. Bowman of Hagensville, Georgia, at Anzio, Italy, in May 1944.

BILL
MAULDIN

When a teacher scolded the young Bill Mauldin (1921–2003) for doodling in class, he responded that he simply couldn't think without drawing. This tendency would make Mauldin one of America's most popular cartoonists—and a vital chronicler of World War II for military readers and civilians alike.

Eager to capitalize on his natural artistic ability, Mauldin enrolled in a correspondence-school course in cartooning as a teenager and later created advertisements for businesses in his New Mexico community. At 17, he enrolled in the Chicago Academy of Fine Arts and diligently sent work to prospective buyers, with discouraging results. Unemployment was high, and war was beginning in Europe.

World War II took Mauldin with the U.S. Army first to North Africa and then to Europe; he was in Italy in 1943 when his work began appearing in *Stars and Stripes*. His

cartoons made him a hero to many military men, who could tell he was on the side of the lowly soldier; his sympathy for "dogfaces"—the slang term for soldiers in the infantry—was clear in his presentation of his unshaven protagonists, Willie and Joe. For civilian readers, Mauldin's cartoons offered an eye-opening look at the experience—sleeping in barns, dodging bullets in foxholes—of American soldiers in Europe. Above all, his cartoons showed the tedium of war; when there is heroism, it is understated. With humor or small acts of kindness, Willie and Joe supported each other in grim circumstances.

By the time Mauldin came home to the United States in 1945, he was famous. He won a Pulitzer Prize "for distinguished service as a cartoonist," and the Allied high command awarded him its Legion of Merit. His work had clearly touched the nation, and celebrated war correspondent Ernie Pyle praised him as "the finest cartoonist the war has produced. And that's not merely because his cartoons are funny, but because they are also terribly grim and real."

MAIL USE STAMPS

PRINTED IN GREATER quantities to meet the varying needs of the public, the U.S. Postal Service's mail use stamps are designed with the same care as each year's commemoratives, but they convey their specific purpose more directly, and often in much smaller spaces. Seen on countless letters and cards and also used by many businesses, these stamps include the Forever issuances and tend to feature such instantly recognizable images as flowers, flags, and holiday symbols. For many Americans, these issuances represent the most prominent public face of the U.S. stamp program, but collectors can attest that mail use stamps prompt interesting conversations—and serve as invitations to a much larger world.

FLAGS OF OUR NATION: SET 4

THE U.S. POSTAL SERVICE continues the Flags of Our Nation series with ten se-tenant stamps that spotlight nine state flags alongside the Stars and Stripes. Most designs include a snapshot view of an everyday activity or scene associated with the state, but sometimes the view is of something less commonplace—rare wildlife, for example, or a scenic landscape. Unlike some previous multi-stamp issuances, this series is not limited to official animals, flowers, or products, nor is it meant to showcase well-known buildings, landmarks, or monuments.

Each Stars and Stripes stamp included in the annual Flags of Our Nation issuances features snapshot artwork inspired by the opening lines of "America the Beautiful" by Katharine Lee Bates (1859–1929). This year, "purple mountain majesties" rise prominently in the background.

ART DIRECTOR AND DESIGNER: Howard E. Paine
ARTIST: Tom Engeman
PLACE AND DATE OF ISSUE: New York, NY, April 16, 2010

MONARCH
FIRST-CLASS SURCHARGE RATE

THE ENVELOPES of many large greeting cards that require additional postage will soon carry an outline of a generic butterfly, a reminder to purchase this new stamp featuring one of the most recognizable butterflies in North America.

Tom Engeman has designed numerous stamps for the U.S. Postal Service, including the Liberty Bell Forever stamp, various stamped cards in the Historical Preservation series, and 60 stamps for the Flags of Our Nation series that began in 2008. For this issuance, he used photographs of preserved butterflies to create a highly stylized, simplified image of a monarch—more the illusion of the butterfly than an exact replica.

ART DIRECTOR AND DESIGNER: Derry Noyes
ARTIST: Tom Engeman
PLACE AND DATE OF ISSUE: New York, NY, May 17, 2010

LOVE:
PANSIES IN A BASKET

VIVID COLORS, velvety petals, and intriguing "faces" have long made pansies a favorite flower of gardeners and artists. Cards and stamps depicting these graceful blossoms convey sentiments of appreciation, affection, and love.

The floral design on this stamp is a detail from a watercolor created by the late Dorothy Maienschein, an employee of Hallmark Cards, Inc. Introduced as a Mother's Day card in 1939, Hallmark reissued the design as a friendship card in 1941. Since Hallmark began tracking sales in 1942, almost 30 million cards with this design have been purchased—more than any card in history.

The Postal Service began issuing its popular Love stamps in 1973. Over the years these stamps have featured a wide variety of designs, including heart motifs, colorful flowers, and the word "LOVE" itself.

ART DIRECTOR AND DESIGNER: Derry Noyes
EXISTING ART BY: Dorothy Maienschein
PLACE AND DATE OF ISSUE: Kansas City, MO, April 22, 2010

ANGEL WITH LUTE

THIS MUSICAL ANGEL was originally part of a larger fresco in the apse of the Basilica dei Santi Apostoli in Rome. The complete fresco included Christ, the Apostles, and several angelic musicians. It was painted around 1480 but partially destroyed in 1711 when the church was reconstructed. The fragment shown on the stamp and thirteen other surviving fragments from the fresco are on display in Room IV of the Vatican Pinacoteca in Rome.

Little is known about Melozzo da Forli (1438–1494) prior to his work in Rome during the last quarter of the 15th century. During the pontificate of Sixtus IV (1474–1484), he was named *pictor papalis,* or "papal painter." Today, in addition to his fragmented fresco of musical angels, Melozzo is also remembered for a circa-1477 fresco commemorating the appointment of the first prefect of the Vatican Library.

ART DIRECTOR AND DESIGNER: Terrence W. McCaffrey
ARTIST: Melozzo da Forli
PLACE AND DATE OF ISSUE: New York, NY, October 21, 2010

HOLIDAY EVERGREENS

NED M. SEIDLER, who died in 2007, created numerous stamp designs for the U.S. Postal Service and was a gifted painter of nature subjects. When painting flora, he frequently used cuttings from his own yard.

Ponderosa pine (*Pinus ponderosa*), also called western yellow pine, can be found across much of the western United States. Its long needles typically grow in sheathed bundles of three, occasionally more, and its pineapple-shaped cones are reddish brown.

Eastern red cedar (*Juniperus virginiana*) belongs to the cypress family and is the most widely distributed eastern conifer. The fragrant, dark-green foliage consists of small, overlapping, scalelike leaves. The fleshy, resinous, blue "berries" are actually highly modified seed cones that attract birds and other wildlife.

Blue spruce (*Picea pungens*), also called Colorado blue spruce, is often cultivated for ornamental use in landscape settings. With its attractive blue-green or silvery blue foliage and dense, symmetrical, pyramidal shape, this native of western North America makes a popular Christmas tree. In autumn, the pendant oval cones turn chestnut brown with stiff, rough-edged, flattened scales. The cones generally remain on the tree a year or two after their seeds fall.

Balsam fir (*Abies balsamea*) is native to both the Northeast and Midwest. This fragrant, symmetrical conifer is a popular choice for Christmas trees and wreaths. Its flat, resinous needles have blunt, rounded tips and tend to curve upward, exposing their lighter undersurfaces. The cylindrical cones stand erect on branches and eventually shatter completely, shedding their scales and releasing their seeds.

ART DIRECTOR AND DESIGNER: Howard E. Paine
ARTIST: Ned M. Seidler
PLACE AND DATE OF ISSUE: New York, NY, October 21, 2010

THE 2010 STAMP YEARBOOK
CREDITS

COVER

(top to bottom) Hulton Archives/Getty Images; © Frans Lanting/Corbis; Artwork by Kadir Nelson © U.S. Postal Service.

INTRODUCTION

PAGE 7 Photograph by Clemente Bogle, Jr./U.S. Postal Service

ICONS

PAGE 8 Digital Image © The Museum of Modern Art/Licensed by SCALA/Art Resource, NY.

ABSTRACT EXPRESSIONISTS

The Golden Wall, 1961 by Hans Hofmann. © 2009 The Renate, Hans & Maria Hofmann Trust/Artists Rights Society (ARS), New York.

The Liver Is the Cock's Comb, 1944 by Arshile Gorky. © 2009 Artists Rights Society (ARS), New York.

Romanesque Façade, 1949 by Adolph Gottlieb. © Adolph and Esther Gottlieb Foundation/VAGA, New York, NY.

La Grande Vallée 0, 1983 by Joan Mitchell. Private Collection. © Estate of Joan Mitchell.

Courtesy Joan Mitchell Foundation and Edward Tyler Nahem.

1948-C, 1948 by Clyfford Still. © Clyfford Still Estate.

Achilles, 1952 by Barnett Newman. © 2009 The Barnett Newman Foundation/Artists Rights Society (ARS), New York.

Asheville, 1948 by Willem de Kooning. © 2009 The Willem de Kooning Foundation/Artists Rights Society (ARS), New York.

Convergence, 1952 by Jackson Pollock. © 2009 Pollock-Krasner Foundation/Artists Rights Society (ARS), New York.

Elegy to the Spanish Republic No. 34, 1953-54 by Robert Motherwell. © Dedalus Foundation/VAGA, New York, NY.

Orange and Yellow, 1956 by Mark Rothko. © 1998 Kate Rothko Prizel & Christopher Rothko/Artists Rights Society (ARS), New York.

PAGE 10 Hulton Archives/Getty Images.

PAGE 11 Nina Leen/Time & Life Pictures/Getty Images.

PAGE 12 (both photographs) Arnold Newman/Getty Images.

AMERICAN TREASURES: WINSLOW HOMER

Photograph © Museum of Fine Arts, Boston.

PAGE 14 (left) Image copyright © The Metropolitan Museum of Art/Art Resource; (right) *Eight Bells*, Gift of John W. Beatty, Jr., Image courtesy National Gallery of Art, Washington.

PAGE 15 (center bottom and right) *Breezing Up (A Fair Wind)*, Gift of the W.L. and May T. Mellon Foundation, Image courtesy National Gallery of Art, Washington; *Blackboard*, Gift of Jo Ann and Julian Ganz, Jr., in Honor of the 50th Anniversary of the National Gallery of Art, Image courtesy National Gallery of Art, Washington; (top right) Bowdoin College Museum of Art, Brunswick, Maine, Gift of the Homer Family; (autograph) Bowdoin College Museum of Art, Brunswick, Maine, Gift of Mr. and Mrs. John Calvin Stevens II.

KATE SMITH

Kate Smith™ CMG Worldwide, Indianapolis, IN.

PAGE 16 Photofest.

PAGE 17 Photofest.

COWBOYS OF THE SILVER SCREEN

Roy Rogers © RR. Fam. Ent. Corp./RR Estate/Trust.

Original Art © Autry Qualified Interest Trust and The Autry Foundation.

PAGE 18 (top left) © Bettmann/Corbis; center: Paramount Pictures/Photofest; (bottom left) United Artists/Photofest.

PAGE 19 Republic Pictures/Photofest.

LEGENDS OF HOLLYWOOD: KATHARINE HEPBURN

Katharine Hepburn image and rights licensed through CAA, Los Angeles, California.

Woman of the Year © Turner Entertainment Co. A Warner Bros. Entertainment Company. All Rights Reserved.

PAGE 20 National Portrait Gallery, Smithsonian Institution, Courtesy of the Estate of Katharine Hepburn.

PAGE 21 © John Bryson/Sygma/Corbis.

HERITAGE

PAGE 22 Artwork by John D. Dawson © U.S. Postal Service.

VANCOUVER 2010 OLYMPIC WINTER GAMES

36 U.S.C. Sec. 220506. Official Licensed Product of the United States Olympic Committee.

PAGE 24 (top) Alex Livesey/Getty Images; (center) Heinz Kluetmeier/Sports Illustrated/Getty Images; (bottom) Alexander Hassenstein/Bongarts/Getty Images.

PAGES 24-25 Heinz Kluetmeier/Sports Illustrated/Getty Images.

PAGE 25 (top): Heinz Kluetmeier/Sports Illustrated/Getty Images; (bottom) David E. Klutho/Sports Illustrated/Getty Images.

THE 2010 STAMP YEARBOOK
ACKNOWLEDGMENTS

These stamps and this stamp-collecting book were produced by Stamp Services, Government Relations, United States Postal Service.

JOHN E. POTTER
Postmaster General, Chief Executive Officer

MARIE THERESE DOMINGUEZ
Vice President, Government Relations and Public Policy

DAVID E. FAILOR
Executive Director, Stamp Services

Special thanks are extended to the following individuals for their contributions to the production of this book:

UNITED STATES POSTAL SERVICE

TERRENCE W. McCAFFREY
Manager, Stamp Development

CINDY L. TACKETT
Manager, Stamp Products and Exhibitions

SONJA D. EDISON
Project Manager

HARPERCOLLINS PUBLISHERS

KATHRYN WHITENIGHT
Assistant Editor

LUCY ALBANESE
Design Director, General Books Group

SUSAN KOSKO
Production Director, General Books Group

DIANE ARONSON
Senior Copy Chief

JOURNEY GROUP, INC.

JENNIFER ARNOLD
Account Executive

GREG BREEDING
Creative Director

ZACK BRYANT
Production Designer

KRISTEN M. KIMMEL
Project Manager

MIKE RYAN
Design Director

PHOTOASSIST, INC.

JEFF SYPECK
Copywriter

PAULA MASHORE
FRANK MILLIKAN
MARY STEPHANOS
REGINA SWYGERT-SMITH
GREG VARNER
Editorial Consultants

MICHAEL OWENS
Image Coordination

SARAH HANDWERGER
MICHAEL OWENS
Image Rights and Licensing

THE CITIZENS' STAMP ADVISORY COMMITTEE

ANTONIO ALCALÁ
BENJAMIN F. BAILAR
CARY R. BRICK
DONNA DE VARONA
JEAN PICKER FIRSTENBERG
DR. HENRY LOUIS GATES, JR.
DANA GIOIA
SYLVIA HARRIS
JESSICA HELFAND
I. MICHAEL HEYMAN
JOHN M. HOTCHNER
JANET KLUG
ERIC MADSEN
JOAN A. MONDALE
B. MARTIN PEDERSEN
DR. CLARA E. RODRIGUEZ